Mastering Live Music Performance: A Guide for Aspiring Musicians

Disclaimer

While this guide aims to provide serious musical wisdom and information, we encourage you to have fun along the way! Remember, music is about joy, connection, air guitar solos, and cowbells!

Mastering Live Music Performance: A Guide for Aspiring Musicians

Table of Contents

Introduction

Welcome to your guide to mastering live music performance! Whether new to the scene or returning, this book is for you. Playing live music is thrilling, blending skill, creativity, and audience connection, but it can also be daunting. This book demystifies the process, providing the knowledge and confidence to shine on stage.

For newcomers, it covers foundational elements like stage presence and basic sound and lighting techniques. It offers a valuable refresher with the latest trends and techniques for those returning. This book provides detailed advice on preparing for gigs, maintaining equipment, engaging with your audience, and overcoming challenges. It's designed to support musicians at all stages of their journey.

Let's unlock your potential with practical tips, professional insights, and inspiration to make every performance an unforgettable groove.

Chapter 1: Getting Started, Finding Your Groove

Start your musical journey by finding your groove. Explore music that moves you and immerse yourself in different genres and communities to identify the rhythms that resonate with you. Enhance your understanding through lessons, seek guidance from mentors, and embrace mistakes as learning opportunities. Engage with the music scene for collaboration and networking and stay patient and persistent. Celebrate progress and develop a unique style that reflects your personality and passion for a fulfilling musical journey.

1.1 Discovering Your Musical Passion

Finding your musical passion is crucial in your journey. It involves introspection and trying out different instruments, songwriting, and musical styles. Focus on what excites and challenges you. Finding your passion will drive your growth as a musician, whether it's rock, jazz, or folk.

Explore music by attending live performances and interacting with fellow musicians. Stepping out of your comfort zone and experimenting with new genres or instruments enriches your musical identity.

1.2 Types of Music Performances

Music performances vary widely, from solo acts in cafes to full-band gigs in large venues, each offering unique experiences. Street performances, jam sessions, open mics, and virtual concerts are also popular. Each type helps you develop different skills, like confidence in solo acts or band teamwork.

Different settings have unique logistical needs. Small venues require personal interaction, while large venues need precise coordination. Street and virtual performances demand adaptability.

1.3 Choosing Your Path: Solo vs. Band

Choosing between a solo career and joining a band significantly influences the path of your musical journey. Solo careers offer creative control but can be demanding. Bands offer shared responsibilities and richer sound but require coordination.

In a solo career, you control all aspects, enhancing versatility but potentially isolating. Bands provide mutual support and a dynamic sound but can face creative conflicts.

Choose based on your preferences and career goals. Some musicians balance both paths, working in bands while pursuing solo projects.

1.4 Developing Your Unique Style

Developing a unique musical style is an evolving process. Blend influences, experiment with techniques, and stay true to your instincts. Embrace self-discovery and push boundaries to make your music memorable. Immerse yourself in diverse musical cultures.

Collaboration with other musicians brings fresh insights. Continue learning through formal education or self-study to enhance your creativity.

Recording your performances and accepting constructive criticism helps refine your sound. Share your work in music communities to gain new perspectives.
Developing your style is an ongoing journey. Your music reflects your growth and evolution, resonating with audiences and leaving a lasting impact. Embrace change and let your passion guide you.

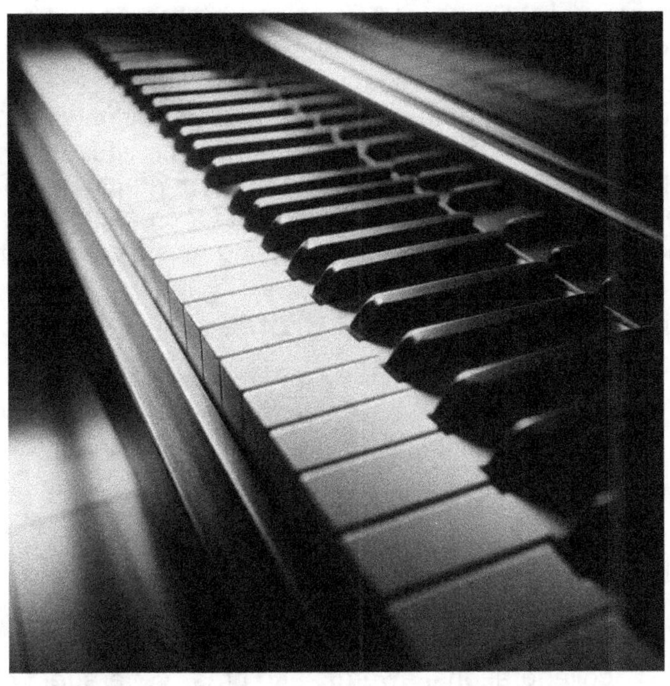

Chapter 2: Using Social Media and Websites

In today's digital age, social media and websites are essential for musicians to connect, promote music, and build a fanbase. Platforms like Bandmix, Facebook, and Instagram help find musicians and establish an online presence, while YouTube and TikTok showcase performances. Regular updates and interactions with followers build a loyal fanbase and boost visibility. A dedicated website serves as a hub with a bio, discography, tour dates, a blog, and an email newsletter that keeps fans informed. Utilizing analytics and collaborating with other artists can further amplify your reach, making digital tools invaluable for creating meaningful connections and a thriving music community.

2.1 Creating a Detailed Profile
Highlight Your Skills:

- Clearly list your instruments, vocal range, and techniques, such as fingerpicking or sight-reading.
- Specify your proficiency level for each skill, from beginner to advanced.
- Mention your ability to play by ear or sight-read.
- Include notable performances, recordings, collaborations, awards, and press coverage.
- Highlight any experience in music production or engineering.
- List your instruments and specialized gear, specifying brands and models.

- Discuss technical skills related to your equipment.

Share Your Influences:
- Mention artists and genres that inspire you to help potential bandmates understand your musical direction.
- Explain how these influences shape your sound and approach to music.
- Describe how genres or specific artists influence your style, encouraging meaningful collaborations.

2.2 Using Filters to Find Musicians
Set Your Goals:
- Define your goals to guide your journey and attract like-minded musicians. Outline aims like playing shows, recording, or improving skills.
- Be clear about your intentions to avoid misunderstandings and ensure alignment.
- Discuss long-term aspirations like touring, signing with a label, or exploring different styles.

Example Goals:
- Join a cover band, original project, or specific genre.
- Detail your creative vision and needed roles for new projects.
- State interest in casual jam sessions focused on learning and fun.

2.3 Creating Professional Profiles
High-Quality Content:

- Post videos and photos showcasing your performances, rehearsals, and behind-the-scenes moments.
- Invest in good equipment or hire a professional for high-quality visuals and audio.
- Include a variety of content to keep your profile dynamic.

Consistent Updates:
- Regularly update your profile to show you are active and engaged.
- Share gig updates, new releases, and notable achievements.
- Engage with followers through interactive posts and respond to comments.

2.4 Using Social Media
Participate in Forums and Discussions:
- Engage with the music community on platforms like Facebook and Instagram.
- Use hashtags to increase the visibility of your posts.
- Follow and interact with influencers, professionals, and other musicians.
- Participate in social media challenges and trends.
- Utilize live streams, stories, and direct messages for real-time engagement and deeper connections.

Social media and creating detailed profiles can help you connect with musicians who share your style and goals. This proactive approach to networking will help you build a robust musical network, paving the way for collaborative projects and personal growth. Embrace the power of digital platforms to enhance your visibility and establish meaningful connections in the music community. By actively engaging with online communities, you can discover opportunities to collaborate on new projects, join bands, or even find mentors who can guide your musical journey. Regularly updating your profiles and showcasing your latest work will keep your audience engaged and attract potential collaborators. Moreover, leveraging social media analytics can provide insights into your audience's preferences, helping you tailor your content and interactions to maximize your impact and reach. The digital landscape offers endless possibilities for growth and connection, making it an invaluable tool for modern musicians.

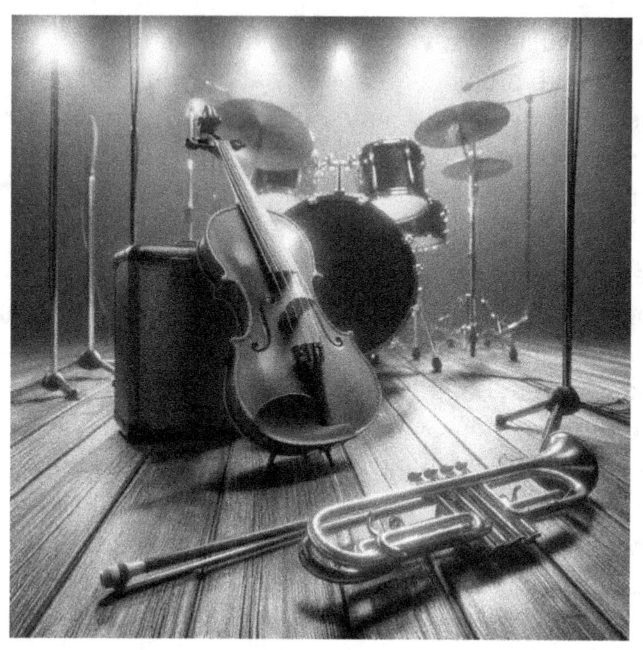

Chapter 3: Setting the Stage by Choosing the Right Instruments

Setting the stage for your musical journey begins with choosing suitable instruments. This decision can shape your sound, influence your performance style, and even determine the genres you explore. It's essential to consider your preferences, the types of music you love, and your practical needs. Whether you're drawn to the deep resonance of a bass guitar, the saxophone's soulful sounds, or the keyboard's versatile nature, selecting the instrument that feels right to you is crucial. It's the first step in crafting your unique musical identity.

3.1 Exploring Instrument Options

- The world of musical instruments provides endless choices, catering to every musician's unique needs and preferences. Each instrument comes with its own distinct characteristics and subtleties. Delving into these options involves understanding their nuances and finding what best suits your style and goals.

- **Try Different Instruments:** Spend time playing various instruments to understand their sound, weight, and playability. Visit music stores, attend demonstrations, or borrow instruments to get hands-on experience.
- **Understanding Roles:** Learn about the unique roles of instruments in different genres, such as the central role of guitars in rock or violins in classical music.
- **Finding Your Fit:** Choose an instrument that inspires you and makes you feel comfortable. It should align with your musical ideas and aspirations.
- **Consulting Experts:** Seek advice from music teachers or experienced musicians to find an instrument that matches your style and goals.
- **Researching:** Use online resources and reviews to gain insights into different instruments and their suitability for various genres and skill levels.

3.2 The Role of Different Instruments in a Band

Each instrument in a band plays a crucial role in shaping the overall sound and dynamic. Each instrument's unique tones and rhythms blend to create a cohesive musical experience. Together, they produce a rich and layered performance that is impossible with any single instrument alone.

- **Drums:** Set the rhythm and tempo, providing the foundation for the band's groove, the heartbeat of any band
- **Bass:** Offers harmonic foundation, supporting rhythm, and bridges gaps between drums and melodic instruments. Bass players provide the
- **Guitars and Keyboards:** These add harmonic and melodic layers, driving chord progressions and solos that define the band's style.
- **Vocals:** Connect with the audience through storytelling and emotional expression, often becoming the band's signature sound.

Other instruments, such as brass, woodwinds, and strings, can add unique colors to the band's arrangement. Understanding each instrument's role helps create a cohesive sound in which each member shines while supporting the collective musical expression.

Additional Considerations:

- **Ensemble Compatibility:** Consider how your chosen instrument fits within different group settings, such as bands or solo performances.
- **Maintenance:** Be prepared for the upkeep that comes with your instrument.
- **Portability and Budget:** Evaluate the practicality of transporting your instrument and factor in costs and potential repairs.
- **Learning Curve:** Consider the time and effort required to achieve proficiency with your chosen instrument.
- **Genre Flexibility:** Choose an instrument that supports the range of music you want to explore.

3.3 Acoustic vs. Electric: What's Right for You?

Selecting between acoustic and electric instruments hinges on your musical goals, personal style, and the settings in which you'll perform. Each type offers distinct characteristics, advantages, and obstacles. Understanding these factors can guide you to the instrument that best suits your needs and preferences.

Acoustic Instruments:

- **Pros:** Natural, warm sound; portability; simplicity.
- Ideal for intimate settings and genres like folk, classical, and jazz.
- **Cons:** Limited volume; sensitivity to environmental changes.

Electric Instruments:

- **Pros:** Versatility; amplification for large venues; durability.

- Suitable for genres requiring amplification and effects, like rock, pop, and electronic music.
- **Cons:** Equipment dependency; complexity in learning and maintenance.

Hybrid Options: Combine acoustic and electric elements, offering flexibility for various settings.

3.4 Maintaining and Upgrading Your Gear

Regular maintenance and timely upgrades are essential for maintaining consistent performance. They help preserve the quality of sound and prevent any decline over time. By taking care of these aspects, musicians can ensure their instruments continue to perform at their best.

Regular Maintenance:
1. **Cleaning:** Regularly clean instruments to remove dust and grime.
2. **Tuning:** Keep instruments tuned to maintain sound quality.
3. **Repairs:** Address issues promptly and perform regular inspections.
4. **Storage:** Store instruments in suitable environments to prevent damage.

Upgrading Your Gear:
1. **Research:** Stay updated on the latest music technology and equipment.
2. **Before buying,** test the new gear for sound and compatibility.
3. **Consider Needs:** Upgrade based on performance and recording requirements.
4. **Budget Wisely:** Plan upgrades within your budget, considering mid-range options.

Continual Learning:
1. **Workshops and Classes:** Learn about maintenance and sound engineering.
2. **Networking:** Connect with other musicians to share tips and recommendations.

Choosing the right instrument is a foundational step in your musical journey, involving ongoing exploration and discovery. Thoroughly exploring your options and understanding different instruments' roles and characteristics helps you make informed decisions that align with your goals and preferences. Proper maintenance and timely gear upgrades ensure optimal performance, supporting your growth and excellence as a musician. By following these guidelines, you can maintain your gear's longevity, allowing you to focus on what truly matters—making music.

Chapter 4: Jam and Open Mic Sessions

Jam sessions, or open mics, are the ultimate playground for musicians where improvisation reigns supreme. These spontaneous gatherings allow artists to explore new ideas, interact in real time, and create magic on the fly. The unpredictability and raw, unfiltered expression make each session unique. It's a chance to push boundaries, experiment with different sounds, and build musical chemistry. Whether trading solos or weaving harmonies, improvisation is essential. Jam sessions are also great for networking and expanding your circle of musician friends, making them the perfect avenue for those looking to join a band or enjoy collaborative music-making.

4.1 Basics of Jamming

- Jamming involves creating freeform, dynamic, and spontaneous music without any predefined structure. Key elements include improvisation, collaboration among musicians, and the ability to respond to each other's cues. This approach fosters a unique and organic musical experience.

  Listening Attentively: Listen to other musicians' rhythms, melodies, and harmonies.
- **Responding to Cues:** Pick up on subtle changes in dynamics, tempo, or chord progressions.
- **Maintaining Rhythm:** Keep a consistent tempo to anchor the session.

- **Understanding Theory:** Know scales, chord progressions, and basic music theory.
- **Experimentation:** Try new ideas and techniques without fear.
- **Relaxation and Openness:** Stay relaxed and adaptable to the music's flow.

4.2 Communicating with Fellow Musicians

Clear and effective communication is key to a successful jamming session. It involves ensuring that all band members are on the same page and understand each other's cues and intentions. This level of coordination helps create a smooth and enjoyable musical experience.

- **Non-Verbal Cues:** Use nods, eye contact, body language, and facial expressions to signal changes.
- **Verbal Communication:** Discuss song structure, share ideas and feedback, and set clear intentions.
- **Respect and Space:** Allow musicians to express themselves and listen actively.

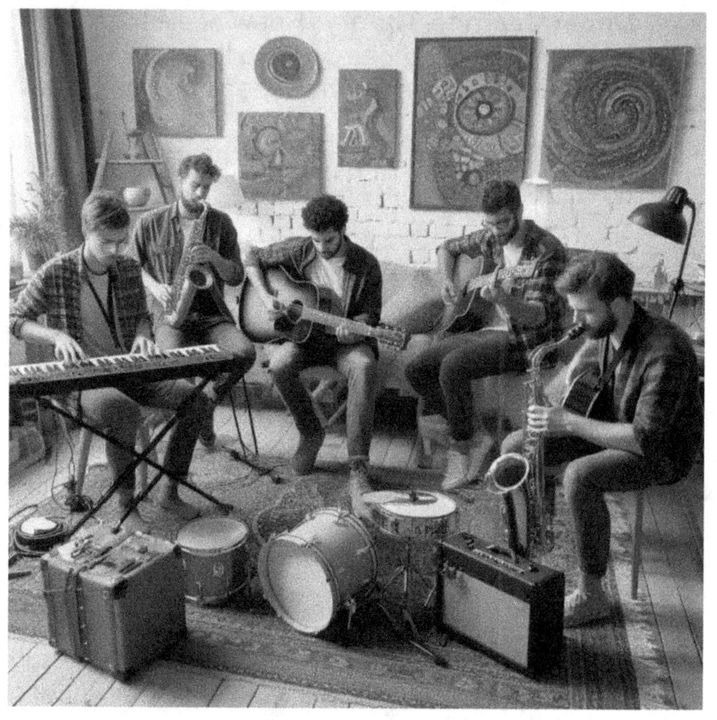

4.3 Techniques to Keep the Groove Alive

- **Call and Response:** Create musical conversations by playing and responding to phrases.
- **Varying Dynamics:** Shift from soft to loud to add emotional depth.
- **Experimenting with Rhythms:** Introduce syncopation, polyrhythms, or unexpected accents.
- **Incorporating Breaks:** Use pauses to create anticipation.

- **Staying Attuned:** Be aware of and respond to what others are playing.
- **Adapting:** Be flexible and ready to change direction.
- **Textural Variations:** Alternate between different playing techniques to add richness.

4.4 Famous Jam Sessions to Study

Studying legendary jam sessions offers valuable insights into musical creativity and collaboration. Observing how iconic musicians interact and improvise can teach important lessons about timing, harmony, and spontaneity. These sessions also provide inspiration and techniques to elevate your own musical journey.

- **1969 Session with Clapton, Lennon, Richards, and Mitchell:** Celebrated for spontaneous creativity and blending different styles.
- **1972 Session at Apollo Theater with Brown, King, and Jackson:** Showcased improvisation, chemistry, and fearless creativity.

Jam sessions are a great way to grow as a musician by:
- **Developing Skills:** Practice improvisation, rhythm, and collaboration.
- **Networking:** Connect with other musicians.
- **Gaining Confidence:** Build stage presence.
- **Exploring Ideas:** Experiment with sounds and styles.

Fostering a good rapport with your fellow musicians significantly enhances the overall experience and results in a more harmonious jam session. The better you understand each other's playing styles and communication methods, the smoother and more enjoyable the session. Jam sessions are more than just playing notes; they are about creating a musical dialogue where each participant contributes their unique voice to the collective sound. This mutual understanding fosters a sense of trust and creativity, allowing for spontaneous and innovative musical expressions. By being attuned to each other's cues and nuances, musicians can create a cohesive and dynamic performance that truly resonates with the players and the audience. The camaraderie built during these sessions also strengthens the overall bond within the group, making every musical journey together more enriching and memorable.

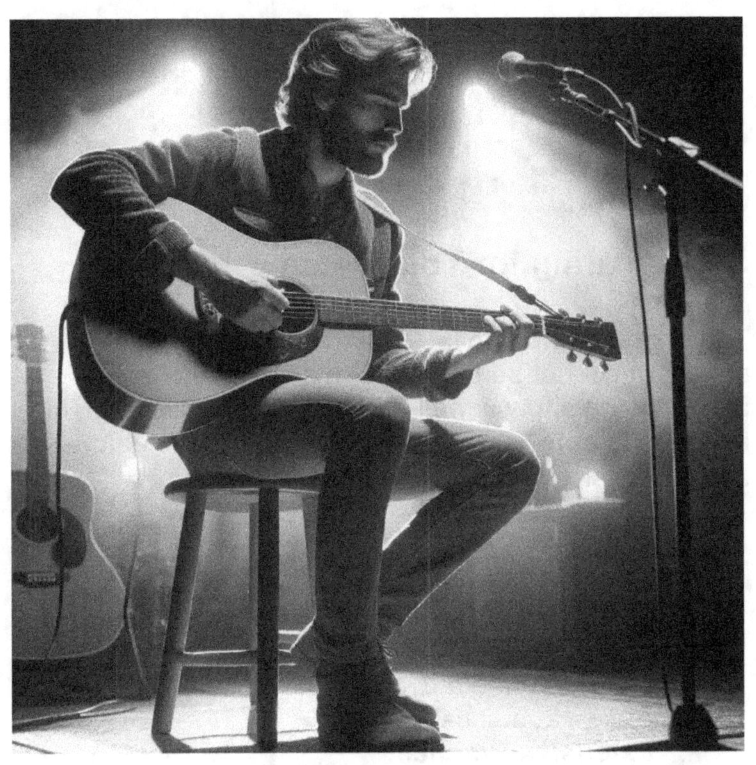

Chapter 5: Breaking the Ice: Your First Live Performance

Now that you've come this far, let's take things up a notch. Your first live performance is a pivotal milestone in your musical journey. It's a mix of excitement, nerves, and anticipation as you share your music with an audience for the first time. This experience will test your preparation and confidence, allowing you to showcase your skills and connect with listeners. Embrace the moment, relish the thrill, and remember that every seasoned performer once stood where you are now. This performance is the first of many steps toward mastering the art of live music.

5.1 Preparing for Your Debut

Thorough preparation lays the foundation for a successful debut performance. It ensures that every aspect of the show is well-rehearsed and polished. This attention to detail helps performers deliver a memorable and impressive first impression.:

1. **Selecting a Setlist:**
   - Choose songs that highlight your strengths and showcase your unique style.
   - Create a dynamic flow to maintain the audience's interest.
2. **Extensive Practice:**
   - Practice each song thoroughly and focus on smooth transitions between pieces.
3. **Attention to Detail:**
   - Fine-tune your timing, instrument tuning, and gear placement.
   - Work on stage presence and body language.
4. **Familiarizing with the Venue:**
   - Visit the venue beforehand to understand the layout and acoustics.
   - Conduct a sound check to minimize surprises.
5. **Simulating the Live Experience:**

     o   Rehearse in front of friends and record sessions for feedback.
6. **Final Preparations:**
   - Ensure all equipment is in good working order and pack essentials.

5.2 Overcoming Stage Fright

Stage fright is a common experience for many performers. However, with the right strategies, it can be effectively managed. Performers can overcome their fears and deliver confident performances by focusing on preparation, practicing relaxation techniques, and maintaining a positive mindset.:

1. **Preparation and Practice:**
   - Know your material inside out to boost confidence.
2. **Equipment Check:**
   - Ensure gear reliability to reduce stress.
3. **Relaxation Techniques:**
   - Practice deep breathing and visualization to calm nerves.

4. **Reframing Nerves as Excitement:**
   - Channel nervous energy into a positive force.
5. **Focusing on the Music:**
   - Immerse yourself in the performance, not on potential mistakes.
6. **Gaining Experience:**
   - Each performance builds confidence and resilience.

5.3 What to Expect on Stage

Anticipate both excitement and challenges along your journey. Embrace the thrill of new opportunities while staying prepared for potential obstacles. This balanced approach will help you navigate any situation confidently and enthusiastically.:

1. **Excitement and Adrenaline:**
   - Embrace the thrill of enhancing your energy.
2. **Technical Issues:**
   - Be flexible and prepared for unexpected problems.
3. **Changes in Audience Energy:**
   - Adjust your performance to match audience reactions.
4. **Setlist Adjustments:**
   - Be ready to adapt your setlist on the fly.
5. **Connection with the Audience:**
   - Engage with the crowd through eye contact and interaction.
6. **Finding Your Groove:**
   - Initial nerves will pass as you start playing.
7. **Valuable Learning Experience:**
   - Reflect on each gig to improve continuously.

5.4 Learning from Your First Gig

Maximize the potential of your first gig by thoroughly preparing and embracing the experience. Take advantage of this opportunity to showcase your skills and make a lasting impression. Remember to enjoy the moment and learn from the experience to improve for future performances.

1. **Reflect on Your Performance:**
   - Analyze what went well and areas for improvement.
2. **Seek Feedback:**
   - Get insights from trusted sources.
3. **Consider Key Aspects:**
   - Evaluate song selection, stage presence, and crowd interaction.
4. **Use Feedback to Improve:**
   - Adjust your approach based on constructive criticism.
5. **Embrace Mistakes and Celebrate Successes:**
   - Learn from mistakes and recognize your achievements.

By preparing thoroughly, managing stage fright, and learning from each performance, you'll build confidence and mastery in live music. Embrace each opportunity and let your passion shine through, as each gig boosts your confidence and contributes to your growth as a performer. Every performance provides new insights, helping refine your skills and making you a more dynamic and engaging artist. Own your stage presence with confidence, reflecting the hard work and passion you've invested. Overcome imposter syndrome by trusting in your preparation and letting your love for music shine despite self-doubt and insecurity.\

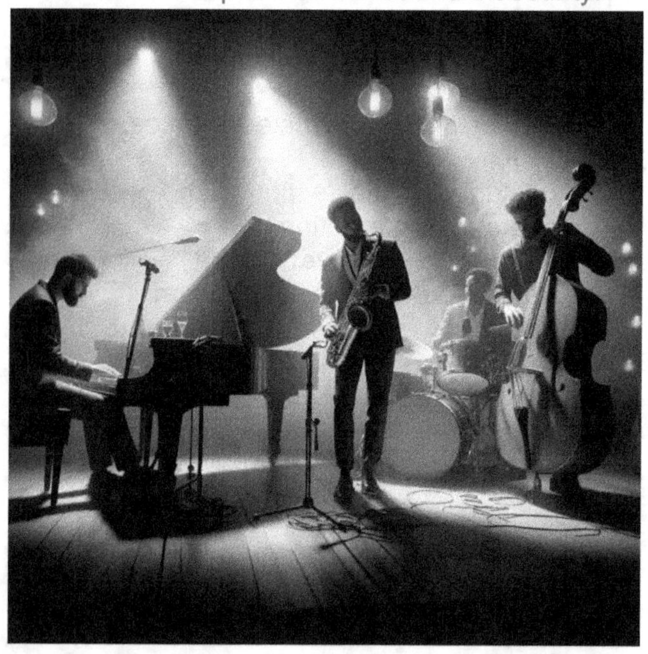

Chapter 6: Building Chemistry: Forming and Joining Bands

Forming and joining bands is a crucial step for many musicians, offering the opportunity to create music collaboratively and perform together. This chapter delves into the essential aspects of building chemistry within a group, which forms the foundation for your collective sound and stage presence. The following sections will guide you through finding the right bandmates, establishing strong working relationships, and fostering a sense of unity and shared vision. You can build a musically cohesive and personally fulfilling band with the right approach.

Additionally, we'll explore techniques for effective communication within the band, ensuring that everyone is on the same page both musically and personally. Understanding each other's strengths and areas for improvement will be key in creating a balanced and dynamic group. We'll also discuss strategies for resolving conflicts amicably, allowing the band to grow stronger through challenges.

6.1 Finding Like-Minded Musicians

Connecting with like-minded musicians is crucial for forming a successful band. Identifying the right individuals involves networking, attending local music events, and utilizing online platforms. These steps can help you find compatible bandmates who share your musical vision and goals.

1. **Attend Local Music Events:**

- Attend gigs, open mics, and festivals to observe potential bandmates and network.

2. **Join Online Communities:**
   - Use forums, websites, and social media groups to connect with musicians beyond your local area.

3. **Use Social Media Platforms:**
   - Create profiles for networking with other musicians, sharing your music, and stating your intent to form or join a band.

4. **Seek Passion and Commitment:**
   - Look for individuals who share your musical tastes and are committed to practice and performance.

5. **Attend Music Workshops and Classes:**
   - Enroll in workshops or group lessons to meet serious musicians.

6. **Explore Music Schools and Institutions:**
   - Contact local music programs and attend student performances to scout for talent.

7. **Collaborate on Small Projects:**
   - Work on smaller projects first to gauge compatibility before forming a band.

8. **Prioritize Mutual Respect and Shared Goals:**
   - Build relationships based on respect and shared ambitions. Discuss long-term goals and expectations.

9. **Organize Jam Sessions and Meetups:**
   - Host or join informal jam sessions to find musicians you gel with.

10. **Evaluate Compatibility Beyond Music:**

- Ensure potential bandmates have personalities and values that mesh well with yours.

6.2 Holding Successful Auditions

Conducting auditions enables you to assess the skills of potential members and determine how well they fit with the group. This process ensures that each member's abilities align with the band's needs and overall dynamic. Auditions also provide an opportunity to gauge the compatibility and chemistry among bandmates.

1. **Clearly Communicate Needs:**
   - Define your band's musical style, skill level requirements, and time commitments.
2. **Prepare for Auditions:**
   - Choose songs representing your band's sound and create a comfortable audition environment.
3. **Evaluate Skills and Musicianship:**
   - Assess technical proficiency, musicality, and versatility.
4. **Assess Enthusiasm and Compatibility:**
   - Look for genuine passion, good communication, and interpersonal fit.
5. **Provide Constructive Feedback:**
   - Offer supportive feedback and follow up promptly with results.

6. **Trial Period:**
   - Consider a probationary period to evaluate consistency and integration.
7. **Decision-Making Process:**
   - Involve all band members in the decision and consider all factors.
8. **Finalizing Selection:**
   - Formalize the arrangement and ensure the new member feels welcome.

6.3 Band Dynamics and Roles

Understanding and defining band dynamics and roles is crucial for smooth collaboration. Each member should have a clear role in contributing effectively. Here's how to manage band dynamics:

1. **Defining Roles:**
   - Assign instrumental roles like lead guitarist, bassist, drummer, etc.
   - Designate songwriting responsibilities and additional duties like managing social media or bookings.
   - Define stage roles and presence for engaging the audience and managing transitions.
2. **Regular Discussions:**
   - Hold regular discussions to reassess roles and adapt to evolving needs.
   - Encourage feedback and be open to role changes to stay agile and responsive.
3. **Team Collaboration:**
   - Operate as a cohesive team, with each member contributing unique strengths.

- Show respect and appreciation for everyone's efforts to boost morale.

6.4 Conflict Resolution and Band Agreements

Effectively managing conflicts and setting clear agreements are crucial for maintaining harmony within a group. Addressing issues promptly and having transparent guidelines help prevent misunderstandings. This approach fosters a positive and collaborative environment for everyone involved.

1. **Establish Clear Agreements:**
   - Define songwriting credits and financial distribution.
   - Set consistent rehearsal schedules and a decision-making process.
2. **Conflict Resolution Strategies:**
   - Address conflicts openly and respectfully, focusing on solutions.
   - Consider mediation if disputes persist.
3. **Building Trust:**
   - Hold regular check-ins and engage in trust-building activities.
   - Encourage continuous learning and ensure all members share a common vision.

Understanding and defining band dynamics, roles, effective conflict resolution, and clear agreements are crucial for building a successful and harmonious band. Each member's unique strengths and contributions are essential to the group's success. Fostering open communication, mutual respect, and a willingness to adapt can create a positive and productive environment that supports individual and collective growth.

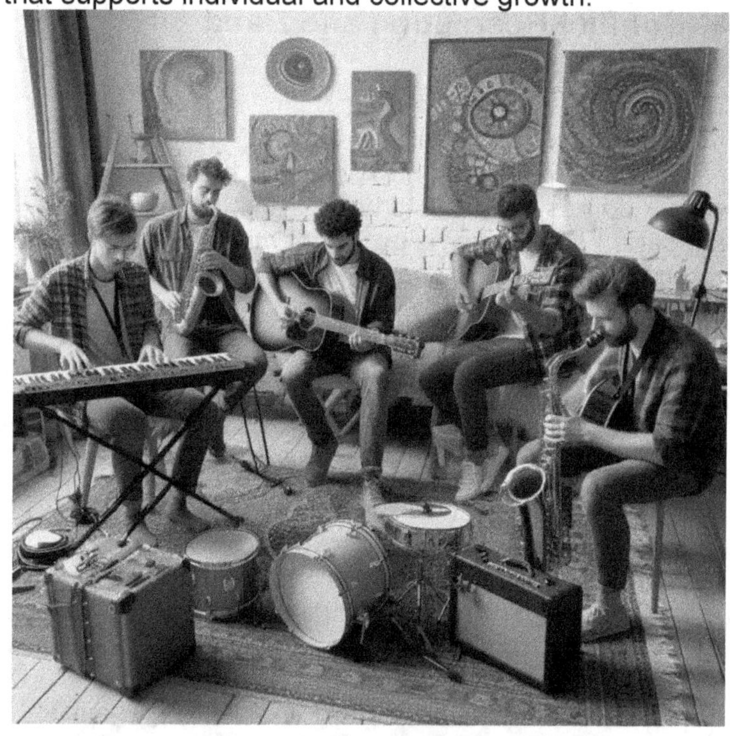

Chapter 7: Perfecting Your Performance: Rehearsal Techniques

Perfecting your performance requires well-planned and meticulously executed rehearsal techniques. Effective rehearsals should be structured, goal-oriented, and consistent, ensuring that every band member is prepared and cohesive. Here's a detailed guide to refine your rehearsal methods to achieve a polished and professional performance.

7.1 Setting Up Efficient Rehearsals

To set up efficient rehearsals, establish clear goals for each session, such as learning new songs or perfecting harmonies. Create a detailed schedule that includes warm-ups, individual practice, and full band sessions, ensuring everyone comes prepared with their parts. Maintain a structured agenda, record and review rehearsals, and provide regular feedback to help members improve and celebrate progress.

1. **Establish Clear Goals:**
    - Define specific aims for each session, like learning new songs or perfecting harmonies.
2. **Create a Detailed Schedule:**
    - Develop a schedule that includes warm-ups, individual practice, and full band sessions.
3. **Prepare Individually:**
    - Ensure everyone comes prepared, having practiced their parts individually.
4. **Maintain a Structured Agenda:**

- Stick to a structured plan for each rehearsal to maximize productivity.

5. **Record and Review:**
   - Record and review rehearsals as a group to identify improvements and celebrate progress.
6. **Regular Feedback:**
   - Provide constructive criticism during rehearsals to help members improve.

7.2 Importance of Practice Schedules

Balancing individual practice and group sessions to optimize rehearsal efficiency to enhance cohesion. Consistency is key, so schedule regular practice times using organizational tools like calendars or apps to set reminders. Set realistic goals and milestones, and be flexible in adjusting the schedule as needed, regularly evaluating and reflecting on its effectiveness.

1. **Balance Individual and Group Practice:**
   - Maintain a balance between individual practice and group rehearsals for cohesion.
2. **Consistency is Key:**
   - Regular practice sessions ensure steady progress and readiness for performances.
3. **Use Organizational Tools:**
   - Use calendars or apps to schedule sessions and set reminders.
4. **Set Realistic Goals and Milestones:**
   - Establish achievable targets to track progress and provide motivation.
5. **Adapt and Adjust:**

- Be flexible and adjust the schedule as needed.

6. **Evaluate and Reflect:**
    - Regularly assess the practice schedule's effectiveness and make necessary adjustments.

7.3 Feedback and Improvement

To foster a productive rehearsal environment, create a supportive space for open communication and feedback. Hold structured feedback sessions after rehearsals to discuss performance and areas for improvement, using recordings to objectively assess specific issues. Provide specific, actionable feedback and encourage a culture of continuous improvement by setting goals and milestones to promote learning and growth.

1. **Creating a Supportive Environment:**
    - Establish a safe space for open communication and feedback.
2. **Structured Feedback Sessions:**
    - Hold feedback sessions after rehearsals to discuss performance and areas for improvement.
3. **Objective Assessment with Recordings:**
    - Use recordings to identify specific issues and visualize areas for improvement.
4. **Specific and Actionable Feedback:**
    - Provide precise, constructive suggestions for improvement.
5. **Continuous Improvement Culture:**
    - Encourage setting goals and milestones, fostering a learning and growth mindset.
6. **Implementing Feedback:**

- Create and monitor a plan to address areas for improvement based on feedback.

7.4 Incorporating New Songs into Your Set

To effectively introduce new material, start by gradually incorporating new songs and focusing on mastering each part before a full run-through. Dedicate specific sessions to rehearsing new material, and test these songs in less critical settings like smaller gigs or open mics to gauge audience reaction. Regularly update the setlist to keep performances fresh, and refine new songs based on feedback and live performance experiences.

1. **Gradual Introduction of New Material:**
   - Introduce new songs gradually and focus on mastering each part before a complete run-through.
2. **Rehearsing New Songs:**
   - Dedicate specific sessions to new material to concentrate on learning the songs.
3. **Testing New Songs in Less Critical Settings:**
   - Perform new songs at smaller gigs or open mics to gauge audience reaction and refine the material.
4. **Adjusting Setlist and Transitions:**
   - Ensure smooth transitions between songs and experiment with different arrangements to maximize engagement.
5. **Regularly Updating the Setlist:**
   - Rotate songs to keep performances fresh and dynamic.
6. **Revisiting and Refining:**

- Continuously refine new songs based on feedback and live performance experiences.

Constructive feedback and incorporating new songs are essential for any band striving for continuous improvement and dynamic performances. By creating a supportive environment for feedback and implementing structured methods for adding new material, you can ensure that your band remains cohesive, innovative, and engaging.

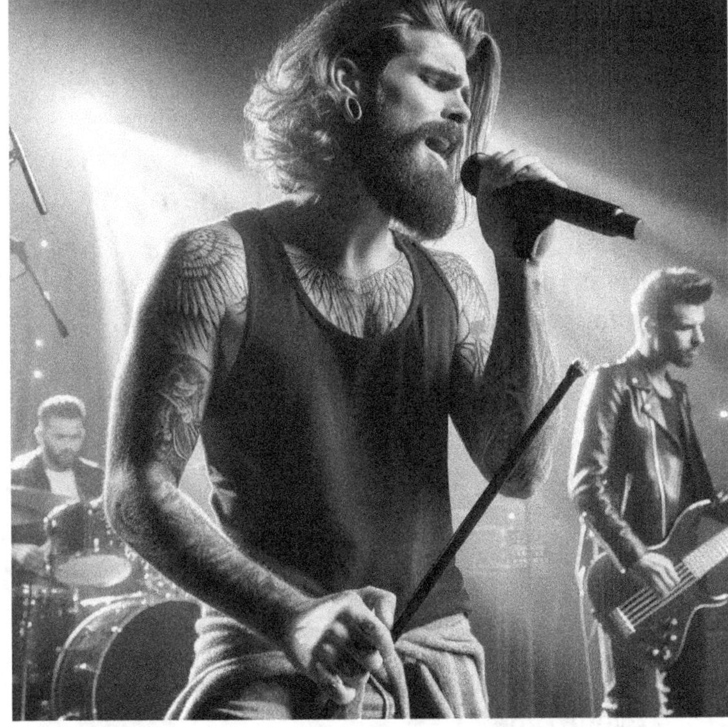

Chapter 8: Reading the Crowd: Engaging Your Audience

Engaging the crowd is key to a successful performance. Connect with your audience, make them feel part of the experience, and monitor their reactions and energy levels. Adjust your real-time performance by changing the setlist, increasing interaction, or boosting your energy. Make the audience feel seen, heard, and appreciated to create an unforgettable show. Tuning into their vibes and adapting can ensure a memorable and impactful live performance.

8.1 Understanding Audience Dynamics

Customizing your performance to suit the audience is essential for a memorable show. Understand the audience's preferences and energy to engage them effectively. You can adapt your setlist and performance style by mastering audience dynamics to keep the crowd captivated and entertained.

1. **Venue Size:**
    - **Small Venues:** Engage with personal interactions and softer dynamics.
    - **Large Venues:** Use high-energy songs, bold movements, and the entire stage.
2. **Event Type:**
    - **Concerts:** Deliver powerful performances with audience interaction.

- **Festivals:** Use high-energy, accessible songs to captivate diverse crowds.
- **Private Events:** Blend original material with suitable covers.

3. **Audience Demographics:**
    - **Age Groups:** Use energetic tracks for younger audiences and classic hits for older ones.
    - **Cultural Backgrounds:** Choose songs that resonate with their experiences.
    - **Special Interests:** Tailor your setlist to niche audiences.

4. **Reading the Crowd:**
    - **Observe Reactions:** Watch for energy levels and engagement.
    - **Adapt in Real-Time:** Adjust your setlist and interactions based on crowd feedback.

8.2 Using Body Language and Movement

Enhancing your performance with effective body language and movement can greatly elevate your stage presence. Utilize gestures, facial expressions, and deliberate movements to convey emotion and connect with the audience. By mastering these techniques, you can create a more dynamic and engaging performance that captivates and resonates with your listeners.

1. **Confident Movements:**
    - Use expressive gestures that match the music's mood.

2. **Utilizing the Stage:**
   - Move around to connect with all parts of the audience.
3. **Eye Contact and Facial Expressions:**
   - Make eye contact to create personal connections and use facial expressions to convey emotion.
4. **Gestures and Posture:**
   - Align gestures with the music and maintain good posture to project confidence.
5. **Practicing Movement:**
   - Rehearse with movement and seek feedback to improve stage presence.

8.3 Interaction Techniques: Between Songs and During Performances

To foster a strong connection with your audience, share stories to provide context for songs and introduce band members, creating a more personal atmosphere. Express gratitude towards the audience and venue staff, acknowledging their role in creating a positive environment. Encourage audience participation through call-and-response, sing-alongs, and clapping while adapting your interactions to be genuine and responsive to the crowd's energy, creating memorable moments of connection.

1. **Share Stories:**
   - Provide song context and introduce band members to connect with the audience.
2. **Express Gratitude:**
   - Thank the audience and venue staff for creating a positive atmosphere.
3. **Encourage Participation:**
   - Use call-and-response, sing-alongs, and clapping to involve the audience.

4. **Adapt Interactions:**
   - Read the room and be genuine in your interactions.
5. **Create Moments of Connection:**
   - Connect personally with the audience through eye contact and stories.

8.4 Keeping the Energy High

To keep the energy high during a performance, strategically plan your setlist by balancing high-energy songs with introspective moments. Engage with the audience and adapt based on their reactions, feeding off their energy. Ensure you are physically and mentally prepared by staying fit, getting enough rest, and employing dynamic movement and expressive playing techniques while maintaining tight pacing. Additionally, use breaks wisely by planning short intermissions and interacting with the audience during these moments.

1. **Strategic Setlist Planning:**
   - Include high-energy songs and balance them with introspective moments.
2. **Feed Off Audience Energy:**
   - Engage with the crowd and adjust based on their reactions.
3. **Physical and Mental Preparation:**
   - Stay fit, get enough rest, and mentally prepare for the performance.
4. **Performance Techniques:**
   - Use dynamic movement and expressive playing and maintain tight pacing.
5. **Using Breaks Wisely:**
   - Plan short breaks and engage with the audience during these moments.

Engaging your audience and maintaining high energy is essential for a successful live performance. Understanding audience dynamics helps tailor your show to different settings and demographics, ensuring a solid connection. Body language and movement enhance your stage presence, visually engaging the audience. Mastering these elements allows you to deliver captivating performances that resonate and create lasting memories. Embrace the stage's energy, engage with your audience, and let your passion for music shine through.

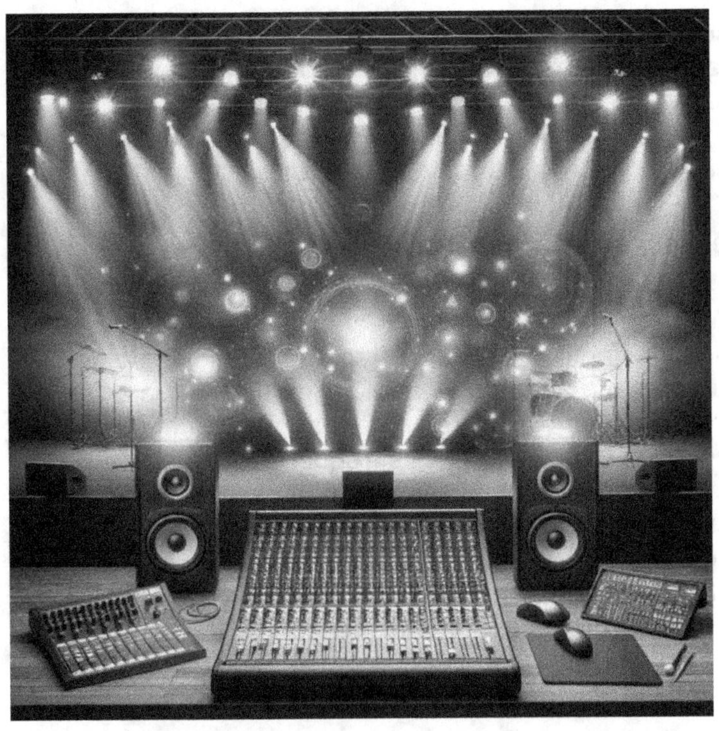

Chapter 9: The Technical Side: Live Sound and Lighting

The technical aspects of live sound and lighting play a pivotal role in shaping the audience's experience, ensuring that your performance leaves a lasting impact and exudes professionalism. By grasping these elements, you can deliver a polished show that accentuates your music beautifully. This chapter thoroughly explores the essentials of sound mixing, emphasizing the importance of working closely with sound engineers. It also covers effective lighting techniques to create various moods and provides strategies for troubleshooting common technical issues that may arise during live performances, ensuring you can handle any situation with confidence.

9.1 Basics of Sound Mixing

To achieve a balanced mix, start by adjusting levels to ensure clarity and that no element overpowers another. Understand and apply equalization (EQ) to balance frequency components and enhance instruments by boosting or cutting specific frequencies. Utilize panning for stereo imaging, judiciously add effects like reverb and compression, monitor the mix accurately with quality equipment, and communicate effectively with sound engineers to ensure the best results.

1. **Levels:**
   - **Adjusting Levels:** Balance the volume of all audio elements.
   - **Balance and Clarity:** Ensure no element overpowers another, maintaining clarity.
2. **Equalization (EQ):**
   - **Understanding EQ:** Adjust frequency components to balance the mix.
   - **Enhancing Instruments:** Shape the sound by boosting or cutting specific frequencies.
3. **Panning:**
   - **Stereo Imaging:** Position elements within the stereo field for space and dimension.
   - **Separation and Definition:** Prevent clashing by panning different instruments.

4. Effects:
- **Adding Effects:** Use reverb, delay, and compression to enhance sound.
- **Subtlety and Balance:** Apply effects judiciously to add polish without overwhelming.

5. Monitoring:
- **Accurate Monitoring:** Use quality headphones or monitors.
- **Regular Checks:** Test the mix on various playback systems.

6. Communication:
- **Effective Communication:** Understand sound mixing basics to communicate with sound engineers.

9.2 Working with Sound Engineers

To ensure smooth interactions with sound engineers, start by clearly communicating your band's sound and specific requirements and discussing your preferences for levels and effects. Respect the sound engineer's expertise by valuing their technical knowledge and maintaining a collaborative approach. Arrive on time for soundcheck, provide detailed setup information, address issues promptly during performances, and offer constructive feedback afterward. Building a consistent relationship by showing appreciation for their efforts will also contribute to smoother soundchecks.

1. Clear Communication:
- **Articulate Needs:** Clearly state your band's sound and specific requirements.
- **Discuss Preferences:** Share your preferences for levels and effects.

2. Respect Expertise:
- **Value Expertise:** Respect the sound engineer's technical knowledge.
- **Collaborative Approach:** Be open to suggestions while advocating for your vision.

3. Preparation:
- **Soundcheck:** Arrive on time and be prepared for soundcheck.
- **Provide Information:** Give setup details, including stage plots and input lists.

4. Troubleshooting:
- **Address Issues Promptly:** Communicate issues clearly during performances.
- **Feedback After Performance:** Offer constructive feedback post-performance.

5. Building a Relationship:
- **Consistency:** Maintain consistent interactions for smoother soundchecks.
- **Show Appreciation:** Thank sound engineers for their efforts.

9.3 Lighting Techniques for Different Moods

Mastering stage lighting involves understanding the basics, such as using spotlights to highlight key performers, wash lights for general illumination, and effects lighting for visual interest. Set the right mood by choosing appropriate lighting, like soft, warm lights for intimate settings or vibrant, fast-moving effects for energetic performances. Collaborate with technicians to synchronize lighting with your performance, rehearse to fine-tune the setup, and explore innovative techniques like LED lighting and projection mapping to add depth and storytelling elements.

1. **Stage Lighting Basics:**
    - **Spotlights:** Highlight key performers and moments.
    - **Wash Lights:** Provide general illumination for the stage.
    - **Effects Lighting:** Use dynamic lights like gobos, strobes, and color changers for visual interest.
2. **Setting Moods:**
    - **Intimate and Moody:** Use soft, warm lights and subdued colors.
    - **Bright and Energetic:** Employ vibrant lights and fast-moving effects.
    - **Dramatic and Theatrical:** Create sharp contrasts with spotlights and color changes.
    - **Ambient and Relaxing:** Opt for gentle, cool-toned lights and slow fades.
3. **Collaboration:**
    - **Lighting Setup:** Work with technicians to design lighting that complements your music.
    - **Cues and Timing:** Synchronize lighting effects with your performance.
    - **Rehearsals:** Conduct rehearsals to fine-tune the setup.
4. **Innovative Techniques:**
    - **LED and Intelligent Lighting:** Utilize modern lights for diverse colors and effects.
    - **Projection-Mapping:** Add visual depth and storytelling elements.

9.4 Troubleshooting Common Technical Issues

To tackle common technical problems, position mics and speakers correctly to avoid feedback, learn basic troubleshooting for your gear, and ensure devices are charged with wired backups available. Preparation is key, so have spare equipment, conduct thorough sound checks, and practice setting up and troubleshooting during technical rehearsals. Build a support network with knowledgeable band members and local sound engineers, and stay calm, using clear communication to resolve issues efficiently.

1. **Common Problems:**
   - **Feedback:** Position mics and speakers correctly and adjust EQ settings.
   - **Equipment Malfunctions:** Learn basic troubleshooting steps for your gear.
   - **Connectivity Issues:** Ensure devices are charged and have wired backups.
2. **Preparation:**
   - **Spare Equipment:** Have extra cables, batteries, and essential gear.
   - **Sound Checks:** Conduct thorough sound checks before the performance.
   - **Technical Rehearsals:** Practice setting up and troubleshooting your gear.
3. **Support Network:**
   - **Team Knowledge:** Have knowledgeable band members to assist with issues.
   - **Professional Help:** Build relationships with local sound engineers.

4. **Staying Calm:**
    - **Remain Composed:** Stay calm to handle issues effectively.
    - **Clear Communication:** Communicate efficiently with your team to resolve problems.

Mastering lighting and sound techniques is essential for delivering a professional and polished live performance. Proper lighting and sound can dramatically transform the mood and atmosphere of your show, creating visually and sonically engaging experiences that complement your music beautifully. The right lighting can highlight key moments in your performance, set the tone for different songs, and captivate the audience's attention with dynamic visual effects. Similarly, high-quality sound ensures that your music is heard clearly and powerfully, with each note and nuance coming through as intended. By mastering these elements, you can create an immersive and memorable experience for your audience. Additionally, understanding how to troubleshoot common technical issues will enable you to handle unexpected challenges smoothly, ensuring that your performance remains seamless and professional. Investing time in learning and practicing these techniques will not only enhance your live shows but also elevate your overall artistry.

Chapter 10: Beyond the Stage: Marketing and Building Your Brand

Marketing and building your brand are essential components of a successful music career. Beyond your performances, it's crucial to cultivate a distinct identity and engage with your audience through various channels. This chapter explores strategies for creating a solid online presence, networking within the industry, leveraging merchandising, and setting achievable goals to guide your career.

10.1 Creating a Strong Online Presence

To enhance your online presence, create professional profiles on platforms like Instagram, Facebook, YouTube, and TikTok, sharing high-quality photos, videos, and engaging content. Consistently post quality updates using a content calendar to keep your audience engaged and employ SEO techniques such as relevant keywords and hashtags to boost visibility. Interact with your followers by responding to comments and messages, fostering a community through authentic and interactive posts.

1. **Professional Profiles:**
   - **Instagram:** Share high-quality photos, videos, and Stories.
   - **Facebook:** Create a page, post updates, and use Facebook Live.
   - **YouTube:** Upload music videos, live performances, and vlogs.
   - **TikTok:** Share short, engaging videos to reach new audiences.
2. **Consistent Content:**
   - Post high-quality content regularly to keep your audience engaged.
   - Use a content calendar to plan and maintain steady updates.
3. **SEO Techniques:**
   - Use relevant keywords and hashtags to increase visibility.
   - Optimize profiles with detailed bios, links, and tags.
4. **Interact with Followers:**
   - Respond to comments and messages to engage with followers.
   - Foster a community through interactive posts and authenticity.

10.2 Networking in the Music Industry

To expand your professional network, attend industry events like conferences, workshops, concerts, and gigs to connect with other professionals. Engage in online communities such as music forums and social media groups dedicated to musicians. Build a supportive network by seeking collaborations and finding mentors, and offer support and value by sharing knowledge, promoting others, and fostering positive, genuine relationships.

Effective networking expands opportunities in the music industry:

1. **Attend Industry Events:**
   - Go to conferences, workshops, concerts, and gigs to connect with professionals.
2. **Join Online Communities:**
   - Engage in music forums and social media groups dedicated to musicians.
3. **Build a Supportive Network:**
   - Seek collaborations and find mentors for guidance.
4. **Offer Support and Value:**
   - Share knowledge, promote others, and build positive, genuine relationships.

10.3 Merchandising and Sales

To develop a successful range of merchandise, offer a variety of items like T-shirts, hoodies, posters, hats, and physical music copies, designing them to reflect your brand and appeal to fans. Implement effective selling strategies by setting up a merchandise table at live shows with friendly staff, using online sales platforms like Bandcamp, Shopify, or Etsy with clear descriptions, and promoting items on social media with high-quality photos. To incentivize purchases, offer limited-time deals and exclusive items for special occasions, and host contests or giveaways while building fan connections with personal touches like signed items or personalized notes and sharing stories behind the designs.

1. **Develop a Range:**
   - Offer items like T-shirts, hoodies, posters, hats, and physical music copies.
   - Design merchandise that reflects your brand and appeals to fans.
2. **Selling Strategies:**
   - **Live Shows:** Set up a merchandise table with friendly show staff.
   - **Online Sales:** Use platforms like Bandcamp, Shopify, or Etsy with precise descriptions and easy navigation.
   - **Social Media:** Promote items with high-quality photos and engaging posts.
3. **Incentivize Purchases:**
   - Offer limited-time deals and exclusive items for special occasions.
   - Host contests or giveaways to engage fans and build loyalty.

4. **Build Fan Connections:**
   - Add personal touches like signed items or personalized notes.
   - Share stories behind the designs to add meaning.

10.4 Planning Your Music Career

To plan your musical journey effectively, start by defining your long-term vision, outlining what you want to achieve in the next five to ten years, and creating a mission statement reflecting your artistic vision. Set specific, measurable short-term goals that break down your long-term vision into achievable steps. Regularly review and adjust your progress based on achievements and obstacles, stay focused and motivated by sharing goals with mentors or friends, celebrate milestones, and create a detailed roadmap with steps, timelines, and resources, using visual tools to organize and track your goals.

1. **Define Long-Term Vision:**
   - Outline your goals for the next five to ten years.
   - Create a mission statement that reflects your artistic vision.
2. **Set Short-Term Goals:**
   - Break down long-term vision into achievable short-term goals.
   - Make goals specific and measurable.
3. **Review and Adjust:**
   - Regularly track progress and adjust goals based on achievements and obstacles.

4. **Stay Focused and Motivated:**
    - Hold yourself accountable by sharing goals with mentors or friends.
    - Celebrate milestones to boost morale and motivation.
5. **Create a Roadmap:**
    - Develop a detailed plan with steps, timelines, and resources needed.
    - Use visual tools to organize and track your goals.

Merchandising and strategic career planning are essential components of a successful music career. Developing and effectively promoting a diverse range of merchandise can create a lucrative revenue stream and deepen your connection with fans. Engagingly showcasing your merchandise through live shows, online stores, and social media can drive sales and foster a loyal fanbase. Additionally, offering exclusive, limited-edition items or personalized merchandise can further enhance fan loyalty and create a sense of community around your music. Collaborating with talented designers or artists to create unique, eye-catching products can also make your merchandise stand out. Keeping track of sales trends and continuously updating your inventory based on fan preferences will help maintain high levels of interest and excitement.

Conclusion
A Guide to Your Musical Journey

As we reach the end of this comprehensive guide, let's take a moment to reflect on the valuable insights and practical advice shared throughout the chapters. This book has been designed to support you at every step of your musical journey, from the initial stages of forming a band to the complexities of performing live and building a lasting career in music.

From the early days of band formation, where finding like-minded musicians and holding auditions are key, to mastering the art of rehearsals and setting up efficient practice schedules, each chapter has offered crucial guidance. We've delved into the intricacies of stage performance, including managing conflicts, enhancing stage presence with effective body language and movement, and mastering audience dynamics to create unforgettable shows.

Further, the guide has provided strategies for building and maintaining a professional network, promoting your music online, and engaging with fans through various platforms. It has also covered technical aspects such as sound mixing, handling stage lighting, and troubleshooting common problems during performances. Each piece of advice has been aimed at improving your musical skills and helping you navigate the business and logistical sides of the music industry.

You can build a successful and sustainable music career by integrating these insights and continuously striving for improvement. Remember, the journey doesn't end here; it's just the beginning. Keep this guide as a valuable resource, and let it inspire you to reach new heights in your musical endeavors.

"I would like to say thank you on behalf of the group and ourselves, and I hope we've passed the audition." – John Lennon

Chapter Highlights

Chapter 1: Introduction to the Musical Journey

- **Overview:** The foundational concepts and excitement of embarking on a musical journey. Setting the stage for the adventures and challenges ahead.

Chapter 2: Choosing Your Instruments and Equipment

- **Essentials:** Selecting the right instruments and equipment that suit your needs and style. Understanding the importance of quality gear and how it impacts your sound and performance.

Chapter 3: Learning and Perfecting Your Craft

- **Skill Development:** Techniques and practices to hone your musical skills. Emphasizing the importance of dedication and continuous improvement.

Chapter 4: Basics of Jamming and Communication

- **Improvisation:** The art of jamming and how effective communication can enhance collaborative music-making. Strategies to listen, respond, and interact with fellow musicians seamlessly.

Chapter 5: Preparing for Live Performances

- **Preparation:** Detailed steps for preparing for your debut performance, overcoming stage fright, and what to expect on stage. The importance of reflection and learning from each gig.

Chapter 6: Forming and Joining Bands

- **Collaboration:** Finding like-minded musicians, holding successful auditions, and building strong working relationships. Conflict resolution and defining band dynamics and roles for a cohesive unit.

Chapter 7: Rehearsal Techniques

- **Practice:** Structuring efficient rehearsals, maintaining regular practice schedules, and incorporating feedback for improvement. Techniques to keep rehearsals productive and focused.

Chapter 8: Engaging Your Audience

- **Performance Skills:** Understanding audience dynamics, using body language, and interaction techniques to engage your audience. Keeping energy levels high and adapting to the crowd's mood.

Chapter 9: Technical Aspects

- **Sound and Lighting:** Basics of sound mixing, working with sound engineers, and troubleshooting common technical issues. Effective use of lighting techniques to create the right mood and atmosphere.

Chapter 10: Career Development

- **Growth and Sustainability:** Creating a strong online presence, networking in the music industry, merchandising, and setting career goals and milestones. Strategies for long-term success and personal fulfillment.

Final Thoughts

Your musical journey is a unique path filled with opportunities for growth, creativity, and connection. This guide has provided you with the tools and knowledge to navigate the various stages of your career, from the initial steps to performing live and building a sustainable presence in the music industry.

Embrace Your Journey

As you continue your musical journey, savor every moment. Your experiences, the people you meet, and the music you create will shape your path and leave a lasting impact. Embrace the highs and lows, learn from each experience, and let your passion for music guide you. It will change your life.

Here's to your success, growth, and the countless magical performances that lie ahead. Keep making music, and let your journey be an inspiration to others.

Thank you for embarking on this journey with us. Now, go out there and create something extraordinary!

If you found this book helpful, I'd be very
appreciative if you left a favorable review on
Amazon. Thank you!

Index of top picks for gear

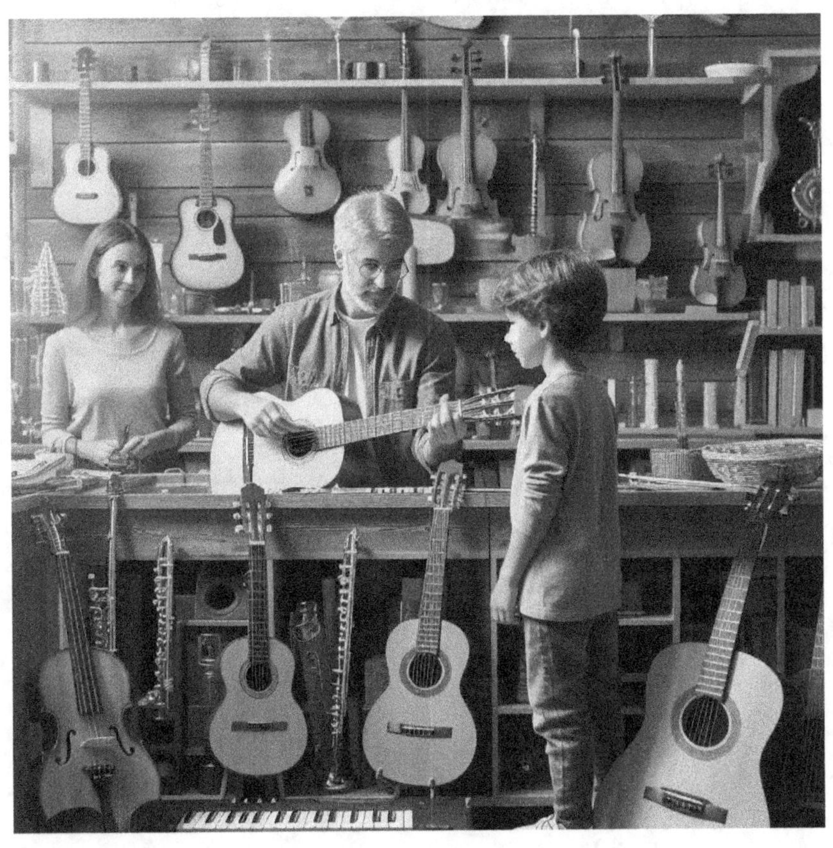

Electric Guitars

Why You Need It: Perfect for rock, blues, and pop with versatile power.
Features: Look for pickups and body types (solid, semi-hollow, hollow).

Top Picks:

- **Fender American Professional II Stratocaster:** Versatile, comfortable, iconic tone.
- **Gibson Les Paul Standard 50s:** Rich, warm tone with sustain, solid build.
- **PRS Custom 24:** Stunning aesthetics, exceptional playability, versatile sound.
- **Gretsch G5422T Electromatic:** Classic rock sound, punchy tone, vintage vibe.

Acoustic Guitars

Why You Need It: Ideal for folk, country, and unplugged sessions.
Key Features: Focus on body size (dreadnought, concert) and wood type.

Top Picks:

- **Taylor 814ce:** Rich, balanced tone, built-in electronics.
- **Martin D-28:** Robust, resonant sound, solid build.

- **Gibson J-45:** Warm, full-bodied sound, durable.
- **Yamaha FG800J:** Excellent build quality, balanced tone.

Bass Guitars

Why You Need It: The backbone of your band's sound.
Key Features: Number of strings (4, 5, or 6), scale length.

Top Picks:

- **Fender American Professional II Precision Bass:** Classic tone, versatile.
- **Music Man StingRay Special:** Distinctive tone, exceptional build.
- **Ibanez SR500E:** Sleek design, versatile tone.
- **Yamaha BB735A:** Excellent build, powerful, clear tones.

These guitars are renowned for their sound quality, playability, and reliability, making them excellent choices for live performances.

Keyboards and Digital Pianos

Why You Need It: Great for classical, jazz, and pop.
Key Features: Weighted keys, sound quality, portability.

Top Picks:

- **Nord Stage 4:** Triple sensor keybed, 120-voice polyphony, enhanced sounds, and dedicated effects per layer.
- **Roland RD-2000:** PHA-50 keybed, dual sound engines, vintage effects, and 128-note polyphony.
- **Yamaha CP88:** Natural wood keyboard, 256-note polyphony, and seamless sound integration.
- **Kurzweil K2700:** Weighted hammer-action keyboard, 256 voices, advanced V.A.S.T. synthesis, and extensive connectivity.

Synthesizers

Why You Need It: Essential for electronic, pop, and experimental sounds.
Features: Sound engine (analog, digital), modulation options.

- **Sequential Prophet X:** Powerful synthesis engine, 8-voice stereo polyphony, and extensive sample library.
- **Nord Lead A1:** Intuitive interface, analog modeling, and advanced arpeggiator.
- **Moog Subsequent 37:** Rich analog sounds, extensive modulation, and versatile performance.
- **Yamaha Montage:** Advanced sound design, 256-note polyphony, and Motion Control Synthesis Engine.

These keyboards and synthesizers are highly recommended for their sound quality, playability, and performance capabilities, making them excellent choices for live shows.

Keyboards for Organ Sounds

Why You Need It: Essential for authentic organ sounds in genres from classical to rock.
Key Features: Sound engine (analog, digital), modulation options, drawbars, and built-in effects.

Top Picks:

- **Hammond SK Pro:** 73 keys, 4 sound engines, overdrive, and multi-effects.
- **Yamaha YC88:** 88 keys, advanced wave memory, FM synthesis, and USB audio/MIDI interface.
- **Nord Electro 6D:** 73 keys, physical drawbars, effects, and USB connectivity.
- **Roland VR-09:** 61 keys, virtual tonewheel organ, 3-band EQ, and Leslie speaker simulation.

MIDI Controllers

Why You Need It: Essential for music production and live performances.
Key Features: Number of keys, pads, knobs, software integration, and portability.

Top Picks:

- **Akai MPK Mini Mk3:** Compact, 25 keys, MPC pads, and assignable knobs.
- **Novation Launchkey 61 MK3:** 61 keys, RGB pads, deep Ableton Live integration.
- **Arturia KeyLab 88 MkII:** 88 weighted keys, extensive controls, robust build.
- **Native Instruments Komplete Kontrol S49 Mk2:** 49 semi-weighted keys, dual screens, light guide, and software integration.

These keyboards and MIDI controllers are highly regarded for their performance capabilities and versatility, making them excellent choices for live and studio use.

Drums

Acoustic Drum Kits: Key Features: Shell material, number of pieces (3-piece, 5-piece).

Top Picks:

- **Pearl Masters Maple Complete:** Exceptional warmth and projection, versatile sound, maple shells.
- **Yamaha Stage Custom Birch:** Bright, punchy sound, reliable for live and studio use.
- **Tama Starclassic Maple:** Rich, full-bodied sound, widely used in the industry.
- **Ludwig Classic Maple:** Legendary sound and build quality, powerful tone.

Electronic Drum Kits: Key Features: Shell material, number of pieces (3-piece, 5-piece), pad sensitivity, sound module capabilities.

Top Picks:

- **Roland TD-50KV2:** Advanced digital trigger technology, realistic drumming experience.
- **Yamaha DTX6K3-X:** Wide range of sounds, excellent playability.
- **Alesis Strike Pro Special Edition:** Combines the feel of acoustic drums with electronic versatility.
- **Alesis Nitro Max:** Entry-level kit with a realistic playing experience at an affordable price.

Percussion Instruments: Why You Need It: Adds variety and texture. **Examples:** Congas, bongos, tambourines, shakers, cowbell.

Other Essential Gear

Guitar Amplifiers: Why You Need It: Amplify your sound for clarity and power.

Top Picks:

- **Fender '65 Deluxe Reverb:** Classic tube tone, versatile.
- **Boss Katana-50 MkII:** Wide range of tones and effects, lightweight.
- **Marshall DSL40CR:** Powerful sound, classic Marshall tone.
- **Orange Rockerverb 50 MKIII:** Distinctive British tone, versatile sound.

Keyboard Amplifiers: Why You Need It: Achieve clear, powerful sound in live settings.

Top Picks:

- **Roland KC-600:** Versatile, powerful sound, built-in mixer.
- **Behringer Ultratone KXD15:** High power, built-in effects, suitable for large venues.
- **Peavey KB 3:** Clear, balanced sound, compact and portable.
- **Alto Professional Kick 12:** High-output sound, affordable

In-Ear Monitors (IEMs)

- **Why You Need It:** Essential for achieving clear and detailed sound monitoring in live performance settings.
- **Key Features:** Sound isolation, driver technology, comfort, and durability.
- **Top Picks:** Here are four top in-ear monitors highly recommended for live performances:

Shure SE846

- **Why It's Great:** Known for its quad-driver design, the Shure SE846 provides exceptional sound clarity and deep bass. It offers a customizable frequency response and excellent sound isolation.
- **Features:** Quad high definition microdrivers, customizable frequency response, and sound isolating sleeves.

Westone UM Pro 50:

- **Why It's Great:** Five drivers deliver detailed, accurate sound with excellent isolation.
- **Features:** Five balanced armature drivers, ergonomic design, and replaceable cables.

Sennheiser IE 500 PRO:

- **Why It's Great:** Natural sound with a single dynamic driver, lightweight and comfortable.
- **Features:** High-performance dynamic driver, ergonomic design, high sound pressure level.

Audio-Technica ATH-E70:

- **Why It's Great:** Balanced sound and clarity with triple drivers.
- **Features:** Triple balanced armature drivers, flexible memory cable, detachable cable.

Budget-Friendly IEMs:

- **Shure SE215:** Clear sound, deep bass, excellent noise isolation, comfortable fit.
- **Sennheiser IE 40 PRO:** Balanced, detailed sound, high noise isolation, durable.
- **KZ ZS10 Pro:** Hybrid driver setup, clear highs, deep lows.
- **Audio-Technica ATH-E40:** Dual-phase drivers, accurate frequency response, ergonomic fit.

Transmitter/Receivers for IEMs

Why You Need It: Essential for wireless monitoring with clear, reliable sound.

Top Picks:

- **Sennheiser EW 300 IEM G4:** Efficient, reliable, excellent sound quality, robust build.
- **Shure PSM 300:** Reliable, dual belt packs, diversity reception.
- **Xvive U4:** Cost-effective, clear sound, easy setup.
- **KIMAFUN Wireless IEM System:** Budget-friendly, includes transmitter, receiver, and earphones.

Microphones

Why You Need It: Captures clear, accurate sound for vocals and instruments.

Top Picks:

- **Shure SM58:** Durable, clear vocal reproduction.
- **Sennheiser e935:** Excellent sound clarity, projection, rugged.
- **AKG D5:** Powerful sound, high feedback rejection.

Accessories

Essential Tools:

- **Instrument Cables:** Durable, quality connectors.
- **Tuners:** Accurate, easy to use.
- **Instrument Stands:** Stability, portability.
- **Strings:** Gauge, material, durability.
- **Capos:** Ease of use, fit.
- **Picks:** Thickness, grip.
- **Cases and Gig Bags:** Durability, protection.
- **Sheet Music Stands:** Stability, adjustability.
- **Power Supply/Adapter:** Compatibility, reliability.
- **Footswitch/Pedal:** Hands-free control.

Music Stores

Along with the big stores, don't forget to support your local mom-and-pop music stores. Your patronage keeps the music community vibrant and thriving, ensuring the richness of our musical landscape.

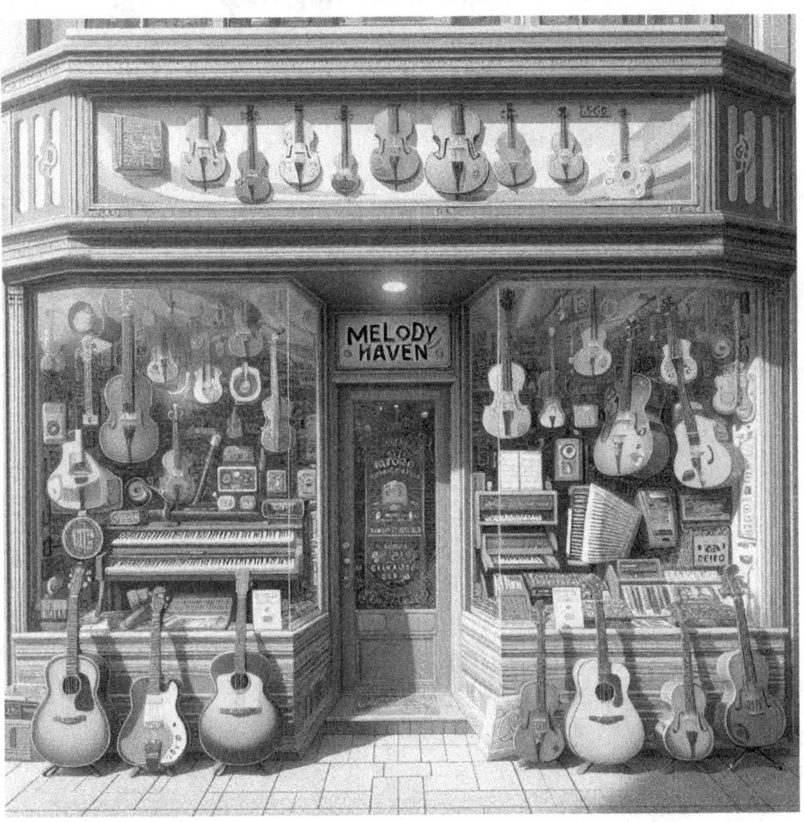

- ☐ **Sweetwater**

  - Website: https://www.sweetwater.com
  - Facebook:
    https://www.facebook.com/sweetwatersound

- ☐ **Kraft Music**

  - Website: https://kraftmusic.com
  - Facebook:
    https://www.facebook.com/kraftmusic

- ☐ **Weisersound**

  - Website: https://www.weisersound.com
  - Facebook:
    https://www.facebook.com/weisersound

- ☐ **Musician's Friend**

  - Website: https://www.musiciansfriend.com
  - Facebook:
    https://www.facebook.com/musiciansfriend

- ☐ **Guitar Center**

  - Website: https://www.guitarcenter.com
  - Facebook:
    https://www.facebook.com/guitarcenter

☐ **Reverb**

- Website: https://reverb.com
- Facebook: https://www.facebook.com/reverb

☐ **zZounds**

- Website: https://www.zzounds.com
- Facebook:
  https://www.facebook.com/zzounds

Resources

- ☐ **OpenAI (ChatGPT):** https://chatgpt.com/
- ☐ **Bandmix:** https://Bandmix.com
- ☐ **Microsoft Copilot:**
  https://copilot.microsoft.com

References

- ☐ **OpenAI (ChatGPT):** https://chatgpt.com/
- ☐ **Bandmix:** https://Bandmix.com
- ☐ **Microsoft Copilot:**
  https://copilot.microsoft.com

That's it! The show's over, folks; let's pack up
and go home!